Learn the Public Speaking and Presentation Skills You Need to Deliver a Successful TED Talk

Jacob Andrews

Contents

Your Free Gift

As a way of saying thanks for reading this book, I'd like to give access to a video that quickly walks you through the major elements of a successful TED Talk. It's a great companion to this book and I hope you enjoy it.

Visit:

http://deepthoughtpress.com/tedtalks

Thanks,

Jacob

Introduction: The TED Method

Since the very first TED talk arrived on the scene over thirty years ago, selected guest speakers have proven a very diverse bunch, including individuals more at ease on stage, such as musicians, television personalities, and political figures, as well as those who come from more typically introverted career paths, such as writers, academics, and scientists. As a result of such diversity TED talks span a wide range of speaker comfort levels, with some individuals approaching it with cool confidence, and others finding it a daunting and potentially uncomfortable prospect.

Now, with TED talks being viewed over two million times a day, they really are being held as the gold standard of public speaking for many people. What this means is that the bar has been set incredibly high, and your next presentation needs to measure up.

Fortunately for you, the ambitious goal of presenting a TED worthy presentation is completely within your grasp! While you may not have the time to commit to the months long process that TED submits its guest speakers to, this book will guide you successfully through all the steps of preparing, and ultimately presenting, an amazing TED-inspired talk.

So where to begin? In the following chapters we've isolated the key elements of a great talk including all components of the planning and presentation process. Remember that while all the approaches that you'll discover in this book are targeted for an 18-minute TED talk, they can also be successfully applied to any other presentation you may be taking on as well. Whether you're new to the game with a big idea, or an experienced sales person seasoning your pitch, these practices will guarantee that you'll make a connection with your audience, whether you're talking to one person or one thousand.

Chapter 1: Find your Big Idea

There's no debate that almost every TED talk you view is impressive in some way, shape, or form. These are highly intelligent, skilled, and often charismatic people projecting their thought-provoking ideas to you as the listener. For some of us this can present a moment of self-doubt. You might see this level of presentation as unattainable, and ask yourself what right you even have to consider presenting at all. Sometimes being faced with someone else's passion can make ours feel small and worthless. It's really important that we refuse to listen to this voice. One thing all TED talk speakers have in common is that they have something to say – and so do you! Some of the most viewed TED talks aren't famous or incredibly wealthy individuals like Bill Gates or Steve Jobs, they're everyday activists who are speaking out with passion about something that they believe in. So what's your story? What is the big idea that you want to share? If you aren't sure, a good place to start is by looking at what makes you tick. What is it that makes you really excited, and how have you incorporated that into your everyday life?

To break it down, first ask yourself this question:

What Am I Passionate About?

It is so important when you're starting to work on your TED talk that you really focus in on what your big idea is. If you don't make a solid decision on a unifying theme or idea, you might find yourself pulled in all sorts of directions. It's important here that you establish the source of your passion. Where do you spend your money and time? What is the major focus in your life? Look at why you've made the decisions that you have, and what has led you to where you are currently. We've all heard writer, speaker, and journalist Malcolm Gladwell's theory of 10,000 hours, in which he posits that 10,000 hours of an activity, hobby, or passion is the equivalent of mastery. This idea of mastery of an area is one that can potentially form the basis of a truly outstanding presentation that can touch many people. So where have you chosen to commit your 10,000 hours (or at least begin them), and why? If you're passionate about something then it is worthy of sharing with others. You absolutely will not inspire anyone if you yourself remain uninspired. Be purposeful, enthusiastic, and passionate, and people will see the meaningful connection that you have with your subject matter. While we'll teach you many tips and tricks throughout this book that will polish your technique, and sharpen your presentation skills, it all begins here – with your passion! You don't want to over think, over plan, or remove all that's exciting about your big idea. When you find something that you're passionate about, your nerves will lessen, persuasive arguments will find their way to your tongue, and the flow of your talk will feel more natural – because it will be. One of the greatest qualities of a successful TED talk is authenticity. You have to appear to the audience as an expert on a topic, someone they can trust, and someone they should listen to. Come from a place of passion and excitement and you'll be welcomed with open arms by TED audiences eager to experience new ideas.

Another way to really hone in on your subject matter, and ensure that you're on the right track, is to make sure that are you really living your big idea. We know that everyone has passion, and each one of us have something unique and special to share, but for everyone that doesn't necessarily translate into a TED-worthy talk. Many of the people with the most viewed talks on TED are people who aren't just talking the talk, but walking the walk. If you're passionate about something t people want to see you living it as well. Most people standing up there on that stage are already out there in the world making a difference. Be great; focus on what you can do, and how you can spread your message in every aspect of your life. Make it a mentality and not just a presentation. People will see your authenticity and passion, and they'll be drawn to you. Talk to people, inspire others, and you will get noticed.

Chapter 2: Is This the Right Talk For Me?

After you've sat down and established exactly what your big idea is, you still need to ask yourself a few questions just to make sure that you're on the right track. While it's wonderful to be passionate about something, it has to also fit other criteria in order to not only be an entertaining and successful TED talk, but also a talk that remains true to you. Ask yourself the following questions about your presentation to make sure that you've hit on something that is going to align with your core values and goals.

1. Does It Embrace My Vision, My Values, and My Voice?

Make sure that your big idea remains congruent with your vision, your values, and your voice. Don't let other people influence you, or guide you toward another idea that doesn't reflect what you wish to be presenting. If what other people suggest to you goes against what you know in your gut is right, then quickly dismiss it. An authentic and effective TED talk should always encompass your point of view, and not represent what someone else thinks you should be doing. This is where you can again tap into what makes you truly passionate and excited. What you believe in? What message can you deliver in a heartfelt manner that will connect with your listeners? A TED talk has to sound like you, and if it doesn't, no matter how well written it is, it won't land in the same way your own feelings would.

Tapping into this can be really important in the first draft of your presentation. Once you've written your draft try reading it aloud while recording it. Make a note of everything that sounds inauthentic, or now how you would say it (believe me you'll know them when you hear them), and record how you would say it if given the chance again. Take this as a free-flowing exercise and don't waste too much time censoring yourself or second-guessing your changes. It's really important at this point that you go with your gut and get down what feels right; you'll have time to fine tune and shine it up before the presentation. Now is just about establishing your passion, your identity, and what feels right for you. Try reading it aloud again and again until you find that you don't need to change any passages. Once you've reached this point, you've made the words yours. This is now your talk.

2. Is It Timely?

While staying true to your own voice is important, establishing that a talk is timely and current is also key when you're attempting to really connect with an audience. Using stats or stories that are tired, overused, or worse out of date, can completely alienate an audience. You want your listeners to view you as an expert in whatever area you're presenting, a visionary who has his or her finger on the pulse of what's happening in that particular field. Referencing material that doesn't present as timely and current can completely undermine your credibility, and you will lose audience confidence. Keep in mind how closely relevancy is tied up into recent and current information, and make use of it. Look for new source material to strengthen your presentation, ensuring that you get the attention and respect that you rightfully deserve.

3. Is It Commercially Viable?

While the purpose of a TED talk is not specifically to sell services and/or products, it's important to keep in mind that it does hold the potential to drive business for you. Anything that scales up your visibility can lead to greater exposure, or sales, or connection with greater resources, depending on your topic and level of exposure. Ensure that you are ready for the potential interest that may be coming your way as a result of your presentation. Whether you are representing a specific group, or letting people know about a service you stand behind, ensure that all systems are go, and that people will be able to find further information, or connect with you, while they are inspired and excited. If there is a commercial component to your talk, make sure that you have the capabilities, and the capacity, to strike while the iron is hot. There's no use in crafting an amazing speech, and reaching out to a large number of people, only to have them lose interest quickly when you don't have the infrastructure in place to support and encourage their interest. Even engaged people can be fickle, and if you don't seize the moment, someone else will. Don't miss out on further opportunities to connect by being unprepared.

4. Is It Consistent with your Brand Positioning?

It is incredibly important to ensure that the TED talk that you want to give is consistent with your overall brand positioning. While it's great to be passionate about a particular topic, you want to ensure that it fits into your general concept of how you want to be perceived both personally and professionally. You don't want to choose a talk that focuses on something that creates a conflict in your life, or isn't congruent with the message that you're sending out. While the point of doing a TED talk is to entertain and inspire, you don't want to do anything that won't ultimately serve your goals. Be thoughtful and smart about choosing an idea that's in alignment with your five-year or even ten-year plan. If it doesn't fit with the direction you're heading, it's not the talk for you.

Chapter 3: Keep it Simple

Once you've focused in on your big idea, and have established that it fits all of your necessary criteria, it's important to zero in on ways that you can distill your talk down to its simplest, most concise, and most understandable form. While you may be passionate about many components of your topic, it's the best course of action to focus on the strongest and most compelling ideas, and ultimately - keep it simple!

Follow these three tips below to ensure that you're on the right track to simplifying and streamlining your presentation.

1. Focus on Clarity

It is really important in a successful TED talk that your listeners can take what they learned from you, and distill it into a few clear ideas. These ideas should be ones that they can both discuss, and pass on to other potential listeners. Don't inundate your audience with a word-for-word, play-by-play of an idea. Make crystal clear sound bites that summarize the essence of your talk. This format resonates more powerfully with audiences, and they'll pass on this simple to transmit information. Don't overwhelm people, or bog them down with overly complicated language that causes them to lose focus. People are looking for your message and your big idea; make it easy for them to find it.

2. Be Concise

While TED talks have a strict 18-minute timeline, it's a good rule of thumb to always run short during any presentation. Having time boundaries forces you to focus your ideas, and that allows you to very thoughtfully consider what content is truly necessary to the talk. Not going over a time limit, and in fact having extra time, shows the audience that you respect their contribution in being there to listen. Taking more of their time than they bargained for can very quickly ruin your listeners' good will, and cause them to lose interest. Not only that, but keeping it short prevents you from inundating your listeners with too much information at once, which can prevent the successful transmission of ideas.

Also, allowing yourself extra time gives you wiggle room to veer off if you need to, in cases where a presentation takes an unexpected detour. Try to finish early so that people can ask questions if something you've said isn't clear to them. Really 18 minutes is the perfect amount of time, and it's been established for a reason, so try to keep that in mind. It's not too long to hold the audience's attention, but it's also a focused enough span that you can make very significant contact. Keep in mind that the minute you go over your time limit, the audience will be watching the clock. You want them to be focusing on you, and not the fact that you're eating into their free time. Set a time and respect it.

3. Tell and not sell

While we did discuss in the previous chapter that it is important to be prepared for a possible commercial boon as result of your TED talk, it's really important to not allow ideas of commercial success to infiltrate and negatively affect your talk. Have all your ducks in a row, but don't make selling your focus. Audiences are looking for solutions and inspiration, they aren't looking to be pitched to, so respect that. Keep in mind that if you provide solutions, a fabulous idea, an amazing story, a great message, or a revolutionary product, then people will want to sign on. If you make that your sole focus though, it might cheapen your presentation to a lot of people. You don't want to lose credibility. Profitability will come if you take your time to focus on being remarkable. Thinking in terms of dollars and cents will only add unnecessary pressure to your presentation. Focus instead on your big idea, or your passion, and the rest will come.

Chapter 4: Capture Interest

Once you established your big idea, and whittled it down to its key elements, it's important to find ways to make what you're passionate about even more interesting and compelling to your audience. Explore the suggestions below to find ways to up your game, and gain greater audience attention.

Cultivate a Competitive Edge

It's true that TED talks are not a competitive sport, but it never hurts to let people know what you have going for you that others don't. While you may have a big idea, you want to make sure that it's not something that's been overdone, or something that people have been inundated with. There are so many creative and interesting ways to approach similar topics, so find your niche and make sure that you're the first person to approach it in such a manner.

Remember, it's not enough to be great at what you do – you have to also be perceived as the only one who does exactly what you do. Just because there are ideas that are similar to yours doesn't mean it isn't worth exploring. Don't abandon your idea that easily! Just be prepared and informed about other takes on similar topics, and find a provocative, interesting, and especially compelling premise that hasn't been shared before. Just because something has been approached, doesn't mean that you don't have a new take worth exploring. Just be sure to arm yourself with what else it out there and move forward accordingly.

Teach your Audience Something New

As a species, human beings love to be presented with novel ideas. Any element of a presentation that is unexpected, unusual, or introduces us to the unfamiliar, will give us a jolt, and push us to think differently about our preconceived notions. This can open up our minds, and make us more receptive to new ideas, which is exactly what you want your audience to be doing during your TED talk. You want to inform, and educate, but you also want to move people and inspire them. Give them something that changes how they see the world and makes them think twice – then you'll inspire them! Along the same lines is the need for your presentation to include moments that elicit a strong emotional response in your audience members. It's one thing to present new information that makes them think about the way they see the world, it's another layer to create fear, shock, surprise, joy, or any other strong emotion in an audience member. Anything that revs your listeners up connects them to you, and draws them further into your presentation.

Be Compelling

More and more we live in an increasingly attention deficit world, and honestly you have very limited time to capture an audience's attention. People are quick to lose focus, and will start taking out their phones or checking their emails before you even get through your first two minutes. Don't waste your time with trite pleasantries that really just pad the beginning of the speech. "I'm glad to be here," and "I want to thank the organizers," are just as boring to listen to, as they sound when you say them aloud. Begin your presentation like this, and I guarantee you've already lost a few potential listeners. The absolute last thing you want to be right off the hop is predictable and boring, so surprise your audience by jumping right into the meat of the presentation. Tell them your origin story, how you found your passion, and what brings you to this stage – and make it good! Tell them something surprising, something that draws them in. In those first few minutes you want to see all eyes on you, not the glow of cellphone lights and the tops of people's heads.

Share a Genuinely Emotional Story

Telling stories is an absolutely surefire way to connect with people's hearts and minds. Standing in front of an audience repeating rote facts, or telling clinical non-stories is only going to leave people disconnected and bored. Highlighting real emotions and feelings will automatically endear you to the audience. If you were sad let them know that. If you were angry, or happy, or felt guilt, or remorse, let them see that too. When you're able to tell stories that express genuine emotion, you are creating contact with the audience.

In fact, brain scans have revealed that stories actually stimulate and engage different areas in the human brain, so cater to that. You might not believe it, but the story that people want to hear is your story! Pull the audience in, get them to identify with you, and let them see your authentic self. Keep in mind throughout your talk that stories are the connective threads that tie us together as people, and allowing the audience inside your personal experience ties them to you. Stories are integral. Tell more of them.

Chapter 5: Frame your Story

While it's important to establish your big idea, and work on ways of grabbing the audience's attention, a successful presentation cannot exist without a strong framework that both conceptualizes, and outlines, what you want to say. It is absolutely integral that you not overlook this part of the process, because understanding your audience, and knowing how to engage people, is all about taking them on a journey. Think of every successful talk as a trip worth taking, at the end of it you want those who journeyed with you to see the world a little differently.

Try taking this metaphor of your talk as a journey, and using it as your starting point. What do you decide first when planning a journey? Where to begin and where to end? To establish where the best place to start is, consider the crowd you'll be speaking to. What do they already know about your subject, are they invested listeners, or are they relatively new to what you're telling them? It can be a dangerous thing to assume that the people you're speaking to possess either more knowledge, or more interest, that they actually do, and if you launch immediately into specific jargon, or get excessively technical, you could lose them right at the beginning of your journey. You don't want to alienate the very people you came to entertain and inspire, so be thoughtful about where you want to begin.

Really successful and engaging speakers are masters are getting very quickly to the point, and not bogging down the beginning of their talk with useless information. You want to briefly introduce the topic, let the audience know why it matters to you, and then the rest is just convincing them to care as well!

Often, one of the key issues that arise when people are presenting their ideas is that they try to go too big, and cover far too much ground. This relates back to previous chapters where we talked about isolating key ideas for the audience. You aren't going to be able to tell the audience everything, and you have to learn to really edit yourself, and what you're going to address while you're laying out your framework. Never try to summarize your whole career, or all of your accomplishments in a single talk. Trying to focus on too much will lead to you missing key details, and from there your talk can quite easily devolve into abstract language and dull subject matter, that is going to eradicate any interest or goodwill your audience has left.

Once you've established a clear starting point, it is important to flesh out the specific examples that you will use in order to get yourself to the desired end point. Limit what you're discussing, and the examples that you're giving, to that which can be explained to the audience. You need set examples that will bring what you're talking about to life, and you need to do it all in the time you have available. Resist the impulse to make broad strokes or generalize. Try to be specific and to go deeper. Give details that add to your talk, and not lose the audience.

While it is important to provide specific details you do want to resist the tendency to over-explain, or to repeatedly beat your audience over the head with the same point once it's already been made. It's really important that you give the audience a certain level of credit, and assume that they'll be able to understand and connect with the information that you are providing. Let them come to their own conclusions, and figure things out for themselves. While providing enough information is key, providing a successful talk is also a fine balance of not overdoing it, and often employing subtlety can be a great tool in connecting with your audience.

Try to think of your talk in terms of narrative structure. You want to begin by presenting a problem or issue to your audience, then follow with a search for a possible solution, and then allow a moment of realization. You want to pull the audience with you throughout the process, thinking of your talk as a sort of a story with intrigue, suspense, and a strong plotline can help do that. Remember that speaking at length about a topic without a strong narrative, can be deeply unsatisfying for your listeners. When there's no progression they aren't pulled in, and they aren't allowed that "aha" moment that's so satisfying to an audience.

While there are many important components to providing a great TED talk, it cannot be overstated how important the framing of your presentation is. Honestly, most times when a talk fails, it is because the speaker didn't take the time to frame their presentation correctly, failed to use proper narrative structures, or generally overestimated the level of interest the audience was putting out. Remember to keep your talk focused on what people connect to. No one wants to hear a listing of an organizations successes and projects; they want to hear about ideas! Present the audience with a compelling idea that they can be involved in, and create a strong narrative. Ideas and stories are fascinating to us; keep the audience riveted from beginning to end.

Chapter 6: Plan your Delivery

Once you've got your framing locked down, it's time to focus on an area where a lot of people get tripped up – your delivery! Use the following strategies and tips in order to ensure that your delivery is as strong as your idea.

Debating Methods of Delivery

While we all have different personal preferences about how we choose to present, there are three main avenues that your delivery can take during a TED talk. You can opt to read a set script word for word, you can develop a set of bullet points that will map out your talk, or you can memorize your entire talk, which means that you'll have to rehearse to the point where every word can be repeated verbatim.

While some people feel that reading from a set script is the best way to approach their presentation, I would advise you against taking that approach. Reading from a piece of paper or teleprompter, will immediately distance you from the audience. People will know you're reading, and this will shift how the audience receives your talk, losing a level of possible connection right from the get go. With this type of presentation any hope of intimate connection is severed, and a formality descends over the entire talk. Relying on a teleprompter or a piece of paper is going to prevent you from speaking naturally and engaging with the audience. It's really best to avoid it!

For other people memorizing a script word for word is the route they choose to take. If this is something that you can take on time wise, by all means try this approach. Try not to underestimate the sheer amount of time that this is going to take you however. Once the speech is written you'll have to rehearse, rehearse, and then rehearse again, to ensure that every word is committed to memory. Consider if this talk is worthy of that investment of time, or if you even have that kind of time to commit. If you don't have it absolutely nailed down, this method can pose a significant issue come performance time. For many people they may feel like the entire speech is committed to memory, and then find a slightly different reality once they're standing up there on stage. This only partial memorization can lead to lulls in the speech, moments that seem overly rehearsed, and lapses where the speaker may need a moment to recall their next lines. There really is a steep learning curve when you choose to present your talk in this manner, and unless you're one hundred percent sure you can nail it, don't opt for this method of delivery. You need to rehearse so many times that the words become second nature. Once you've established that, you can focus on imbuing the talk with passion and authenticity. If you put the time in, you will get there!

If however, this is slightly too exhaustive time and energy wise for you, I would recommend opting for bullet points on note cards. Have a strong idea of your script, and use the points as markers to get you from one point to another. This will provide you with a solid structure, while not tying you so tightly to a verbatim repeat of the speech, that you'll get thrown off if you lose your place or drop a line. For some people this really is the best way to go as it allows an ease of dialogue that the other two methods don't. Focus on your transitions and stick to your general script and you'll be fine.

Pay Attention to your Tone

Tone is incredibly important when you're focusing on your TED talk delivery. Hitting on the right tone can create an immediate connection with your audience. Conversely, misreading the crowd and presenting yourself in a certain light can have the opposite effect, and lead the audience to lose focus on you right at the beginning. While some speakers may feel that it's important that they project an aura of authority or power, that can often feel forced and be off putting for the audience. The key with tone is to always aim for the conversational. Don't force it, don't try to hard to impress, and focus on being your authentic self. In previous chapters we mentioned that a successful talk is like a journey, so be respectful of your travelling companions! While it's only an 18-minute trip, it's going to feel a lot longer if you annoy your audience right out of the gate. Try to be open and conversational, and really make an effort not to project massive ego or condescension. Don't talk down to the audience, if you do, you will lose them. Don't let that happen.

It's Not About the Slides

While we'll address multimedia in a more in-depth manner in a later chapter, it's important that we mention it here regarding delivery. Keep in mind that you are the focus of this talk. It is your strong narrative, your authenticity, and your compelling words that are carrying this presentation – it is absolutely not about the slides! Audiences want to be connected with, and spoken directly to. They don't want to be redirected to a slide that really only reinforces what's coming out of your mouth. Now don't take this to mean that slides are detrimental to your presentation, that is not what I'm saying at all. In fact, lots of TED talks make use of slides.

When used thoughtfully they can enhance a talk, and not break the connection between the audience and the speaker. We only mention it here so that you know that they are not an integral part to a successful talk. You absolutely don't need them to keep an audience's attention. In fact, in a world of information overload and constant visual stimuli, sometimes a passionate speaker with a strong narrative is enough to hold the moment. Use your words to help your audience on the journey, and don't underestimate the power of your voice, and your passion.

Fascination Cannot be Faked

This idea of passion is one that we return to again and again when we're talking about what makes a successful TED talk. We all know that you can go through the motions and artificially mimic all the markers of enthusiasm. You can set the right tone, perfect your pace, and calculate the rise and fall of your excitement. But really you're just going through the motions, and it will be obvious to many of your audience members. The truth is that real excitement, and genuine fascination with your topic is something that is hard to fake, and when it's authentic it can be amazingly contagious! When you waste time faking it, staying removed, and calculating your next step, you aren't really allowing yourself to be on the journey with your audience. What makes so many TED talks amazing is the speaker's ability to allow themselves to get lost right there with the audience. If you're presenting a TED talk it should be on a topic that gets you excited, so let the audience see that. Be earnest, marvel along with them, and talk out your feelings. You spend so much time setting the framework, and finding the right words to make your speech amazing; shouldn't you spend a little time focusing on why you chose this topic in the first place? Find what fascinates you about what you're presenting and really commit to it. You want to share your idea in the hopes that it will grow and spread. Use this talk as an opportunity to do just that! Take the audience on a journey, and make them see the world a little differently at the end of it.

Chapter 7: Master Multimedia

With so much technology right at our fingertips, it can feel almost necessary to rely on it during your TED talk. At the very least you may think that you need slides, and in some cases video clips and other multimedia may seem a simple way to enhance what you're presenting. It's really important however that you focus on keeping it simple, and not bring down an otherwise strong presentation with overuse, or misuse, of multimedia elements.

A key thing (as obvious as it may seem) is to

remember to never use multimedia as a substitute for notes. For example, don't rely on a Powerpoint presentation to lead you through your presentation. Technology can fail, and you really don't want to be standing up there with no framework to follow if something goes wrong. Any multimedia that you use should only enhance the presentation, not be absolutely integral. As we mentioned in the previous chapter, many of the best TED talks don't rely on slides at all, and this is because many talks just don't require them, so there's no purpose to integrating them into the talk. Know your topic well enough to make a solid decision about what works for you.

For many speakers though, using slides and multimedia thoughtfully can enhance an already strong talk. Photographers, artists, designers, and other similar professions may find it beneficial to incorporate strong visual images into their presentations. With these speakers it may be harder to conjure a narrative without strong visual support, and this makes sense for them. When used well slides can effectively support the framing and pace of a talk, and can keep speakers on task, preventing them from getting lost in jargon or incredibly esoteric and intellectual language that can alienate the audience. Things like art and photography can be really difficult to talk about without visuals, and so in these instances (and other similar topics) it can be beneficial to have slides on an automatic timer that change throughout your talk. This keeps your pace, and keeps the audience engaged in your topic.

When using (or deciding to use) multimedia in your presentation, consider these tips and tricks:

- ***Make Sure Not to Overload your Slides –*** Keep in mind this simple rule of thumb when you're using slides. Ensure that your font size is double the average age of your audience members. In a general sense that means that your fonts should be between 60 and 80 points. This makes them clear and readable for your audience. If you're finding this is difficult to accommodate, it means that your message isn't tight enough. You shouldn't need so much information on the slide. Go back to the drawing board.

- ***Don't Ever Read your Slides Aloud –*** Once the information you're presenting is up there on a slide, do not under any circumstances read it to the audience. Make the assumption that they have been able to scan the information and take it in. Your slides should only serve to accentuate your point; they should never be your point! If you read them aloud you are definitely going to lose the interest of your audience, and break the connection, as you duplicate information. Much in the way that reading from a teleprompter creates a disconnect, so does reading directly from your slides. Reading slides aloud makes your words lose novelty, which directly works against your attempts to keep your presentation lively and interesting for your audience members.

- *Use Videos Properly –* While vides can be an amazing tool for certain speakers, they can also clutter up a perfectly good TED talk. Keep in mind that a video clip needs to be short, think under a minute or you risk losing people. Avoid anything that seems overly self-promotional or corporate, as people are experts at tuning things like that out. Be careful with soundtrack use as well, as what may be appealing to you, can be very off putting for someone else who may otherwise have really enjoyed your talk.

- *Favor Images over Text* – I'm not saying that Power Point is the enemy, but it is fair to say that the speakers who are using it to create bullet point heavy presentations are seriously abusing it. The best multimedia support doesn't come in the form of text heavy slides or bullet points. Focus instead on pictures, animation, and videos, with only limited amounts of text. Often accompanying an idea with an image makes it more likely that we'll recall the desired information. Don't meddle with the transmission but leaning too heavily on text in your visual presentation component.

- *Be Prepared* – It is really important when you're incorporating multimedia that you do all your prep work beforehand. Don't wait until you're onstage to ensure your lighting, remote, or slides are present and in order. Talk ahead of time to anyone who might be assisting you with the visual components, and briefly discuss a course of action if something fails.

- *Let the Visuals Speak for Themselves* – If you are intending to use visuals in your presentation try to use them in a way that reinforces what you're speaking about, but also give them time to shine. Especially if you are an artist or photographer, it is key that you allow the audience a little time with your images. Try to use silence in a few well thought out places so the audience has the opportunity to look at what you're presenting. Don't talk over the slides, or try to fill space or time while they are up there. Letting them speak for themselves can often have a powerful effect on your audience. Make sure at this point that you're not retreating into abstract or conceptual language. Let the images do the talking.

While multimedia is something to be used thoughtfully, when done well it can help you as a presenter, bring the audience on a creative and remarkable journey. But remember to keep it simple and compelling. Don't focus on aides that will only serve to hamper your presentation, and distract the audience from what is truly important – your passion!

Chapter 8: Find your Style

It is important to remember when you get up there on that stage, that successful talks are given by people from all walks of life, spanning all types of professions. When TED originally started there was a majority of talks that focused on the worlds of technology, design, and entertainment, but the scope has definitely broadened since then. The important thing is that you, no matter what your focus, find a way to be comfortable on stage and interacting with the audience, this can be done by focusing on a few key style areas, which we'll discuss below.

Pick your Persona

Regardless of what your area of expertise is, it's important to establish what your dominant mission is for doing this talk, as that will inform how you present. Are you there merely to entertain, educate, or inspire. Figuring out what your purpose is can help you understand how much information, humour, or emotion should be injected into your presentation. By no means does this mean you have to fit yourself into a box, it just means you'll approach your talk from a certain type of perspective. Educators such as academics and engineers may approach from a more technical, info-based place. Entertainers such as television personalities and comedians may rely heavily on humour and the tricks of their trade, while activists and people with a cause may focus heavily on their passion and their desire to incite action. You can definitely focus on mixing a blend of approaches, but establishing what your goal and focus is, can really help you streamline your energy, and better connect with the audience.

Being Comfortable on Stage

For many inexperienced presenters, often the most difficult part of giving a presentation is the physical act of being on stage. What they should keep in mind however is that many presenters overestimate the importance of the element of stage presence. We're not saying it's not important, but know that your speech won't be made or broken because of a little on stage nervousness. Ultimately your speech will succeed or fail based on your words, your story, and the substance behind your presentation, but it never hurts to deliver it all confidently. Luckily, this is something that can be coached, and with a few simple body language tips you're already on your way to presenting in a strong, confident manner. Here are two major things to focus on to get you started.

- **Don't Move Too Much –** One of the biggest mistakes that inexperienced presenters make it moving around too much. Often you'll see them swaying from side to side or shifting weight back and forth from right leg to left. This is a natural response to nervousness, but it really does distract the audience, and may display a hesitation or discomfort that audiences might find off-putting. When in doubt, make a conscious effort to keep your lower body motionless. If walking around the stage is something that comes naturally to you, by all means do it! But, for the vast majority of people your safest default is standing still and using hand gestures to create the emphasis that you want.

- **Make Eye Contact** – Probably the most important thing we can impress upon a novice presenter is the absolutely key component of making eye contact. This is a surefire way to connect with your audience, engaging them in your words. Refusing to look at them allows their minds to roam, and really locking eyes with the audience ensures that the points of your talk are landing effectively. Try to find a few friendly faces in the audience, or people who look engaged and receptive. When in doubt revert to them. If you're looking at them you're not staring at your script, or a teleprompter. You're making an effort to really forge a connection with your audience.

Face Your Fears

While being conscious of your body language and bearing on stage is an excellent ways to make sure that you're dealing with your nervousness, know that it is absolutely nothing to be ashamed of. Nerves don't have to be the disaster you anticipate if you face them and deal with them proactively. Remember that the audience fully expects you to be nervous. In fact, nerves are really just a natural body response that can actually improve your performance imbuing you with a sense of energy and a sharpened mind. Engage these tricks to assuage nervousness and stay focused on your talk.

- **Breathe Deeply –** Take deep controlled breaths before you go on stage. Doing this will calm you down and relax your nervous system. You want to be as calm as possible before you delve into your presentation. Focused breathing during your talk may also help you in moments of stress, such as when you forgot your next point, or a slide doesn't work as you had planned.

- **Acknowledge your Nerves –** While not a tactic that can be used by everyone, actually acknowledging your nervousness can create engagement with your audience. People are incredibility receptive to vulnerability, especially if it connects with your topic on an emotional level. People will often react to vulnerability with compassion, and by rooting for a person, but this will only work if it's the right kind of talk, and if the vulnerability is authentic. Keep in mind there are biological reasons why we fear being noticed by a group, because a lot of responsibility comes with speaking up, and for some people that is really difficult. Strangely, the struggle of that unfolding in front of an audience can often be very engaging and beautiful. The best communicators allow themselves to be vulnerable; so don't be afraid to do the same if it feels natural to you.

- **Focus on Speaking Slowly** – Often our tendency when we're nervous is to race quickly through information in order to lessen the amount of time we have to up on stage, vulnerable and nervous. Fast-talking is often associated with trying to pull something over on someone (like the car salesman stereotype), and not actually having the information to back up the claims. Taking the time to slow down and clearly articulate your points, will not only create a calming pace for you as a presenter, it also reads as more

trustworthy and educated to the
audience.

Focus On Earning Attention

It's important when we're starting to plan our
presentation style that we really focus on the
things we should and should not be doing. Don't
just assume the audience will give you their
attention; you really need to work for it. Make
your presentation so interesting, inspiring, and
entertaining, that their phones will go unnoticed.
Remember it's your job to make them listen, and
with the following tips you'll be well on your way
to doing just that.

- **Use Questions –** One way that many
  speakers attempt to engage the audience
  is by skillful use of questions. You want to
  awaken your audience by getting them in
  the mindset of thinking and questioning.
  It's not overly important what the
  questions are, though of course they
  should relate to the content of your talk.
  The questions really are jus the vehicle to
  guide the audience into the talk, and
  move them from broad and conceptual
  ideas into the more specific. Think of it as
  a gradual on-ramp for the audience.

Another great technique is to ask the audience a question they can't answer, and let them know that you don't necessarily have the answer either. Explain to them why you don't have the answer, but let them know what you do know. Most speakers claim to have the answer, the fact that you willingly admit you don't, both humanizes you, and makes you vulnerable. These two things will ultimately endear you to the audience.

- **Get your Listeners in the Mindset** – This works along the same lines as the use of questions, in that it's about engaging your audience and bringing them into your talk. Keep in mind that a well-constructed story, or an interesting fact, can also be a good attention getter that will serve to frame the speech.

- **Choose your Wording** - Once you've gotten a handle on your nerves is can be very helpful to your presentation if you really take the time to think about how the information that you'll be sharing should be transmitted, in order that it be received in the way that you desire. Keep in mind that humans are wired to be more responsive to information transmitted in certain way. For example when I say to you "let me tell you a story about that." I'm phrasing it as if it's something you desire, almost a reward, and your brain will respond favorably to that.

- ***Use Humor (But Don't Feel the Need to Crack Jokes)*** – As human beings we're wired to be receptive to things that make us laugh or bring us joy. When someone makes us chuckle we automatically label them more likeable, and therefore we're more open to speaking with, and listening to them. Keep in mind though that you don't need to crack an endless string of jokes to use humor in your presentation. There are numerous ways to amuse your audience including using self-deprecating humor, or delivering amusing anecdotes or observations about your chosen field (if you're a scientists make a few nerd cracks). Humorous anecdotes of any nature will be beneficial if you work them into your talk, especially if you're dealing with a heavier subject matter. Jokes can lighten levity in moments when you need it, and it can keep people from being desensitized to your message. Endear yourself to the audience with a few well-thought out uses of humor.

- ***Always Repeat Yourself*** - While we're sure that everything you're saying is earth shattering and amazing, we can guarantee that the audience (no matter how interested) hasn't absorbed every single word. That's why it doesn't hurt to create a structure in which you can repeat and reinforce key points in a way that doesn't make the audience feel condescended to. Let them know that you understand they may already have a concept of what you're saying using "as I mentioned," or "you'll remember from earlier." Don't talk down to them, but gently remind them of what points you're trying to get across. It will serve to reinforce the information that you're sharing. So repeat away!

- ***Understand your Inflection Point*** – In every speech there is a point in which the journey turns in on itself, and this is called the inflection point. From here your tone will change, the focus will shift slightly, and in most cases there's a set line of dialogue on which this all hinges. These inflection points could include a discovery that you made that answers the question you've posited in the beginning of the speech, or it could be in reference to a change of world view that you've have. It is incredibly important that you're able to find this part of your speech, and understand how best to emphasize and express it for the audience. This is a turning point, a moment where the speech begins to come together and you reveal what the audience has been waiting for – so use this part wisely. Give yourself space, and make sure to really emphasize when you deliver it. Let the audience know this is the big moment, and then proceed to back it up with fact, personal narrative, and solid information. This is when you have them reeled in, so make sure they stay hooked with tangible, significant material. Remember that clear examples, data points, and scientific research will all function as proof points to build a foundation that strongly supports your primary message.

- ***Work on Pacing and Pauses*** – While we encouraged you in this chapter to focus on speaking slowly to not lose your audience, finding a way to map pace and tone is more complicated than just speaking slowly or quickly. You want to make sure that your presentation works in a series of peaks and valleys to draw your audience in, and build a rapport.

Keep in mind however that speed of pace isn't nearly as important as making use of carefully planned breaks. If you're naturally a fast speaker it's a good idea to try to rein it in a little. Try to avoid losing the audience. However, you can also use the natural rhythms of your voice to your advantage, and train yourself to reveal information in a thoughtful, well-paced way. One way to do this is by chunking information. Chunking is essentially a forced break in your speech at planned intervals. With this technique a pause is necessary before moving on to the next piece of information. You don't however want to abuse or misuse pauses. It can be annoying to watch a presentation where the speaker overuses the dramatic pause, as it loses a bit of its flair after the fortieth time it's made use of. A good rule of thumb when building in pauses is to isolate key points that you think would make great "aha" moments, or sound bites, and work your pauses around those. In this modern age people are constantly sharing the pearls of wisdom from TED talks online, and on their social media. Identity those moments in your speech, and isolate them for the listener. Make sure also that when you build in a pause it's significant enough that the audience understands what you're doing, and doesn't just think you lost your place. Under five seconds they may not quite get it, over five and they'll understand that it was intentional. Learn to be comfortable with incorporating a little bit of silence, as confident speakers use pauses very effectively for their own purposes.

- ***Play with Parallel Structure*** – A really great tactic to use in your presentation is parallel structure. This is a stylistic choice that creates a lovely rhythm in your speech. To use it you repeat a series of words or phrases that sound similar in cadence and construction. Employing contrast is a type of parallel structure. An example of this is the famous John F. Kennedy line, "Ask not what your country can do for you. Ask what you can do for your country." The repetition of the words in both the first and second line creates balance, while it makes the speech memorable and impactful. You can play with this idea throughout your speech, but be sure not to overuse it. You need to reserve it for parts of your presentation where you want to make the most impact. It's a wonderful tactic, but use it wisely.

- ***Don't Make Excuses*** – We've focused a lot on the things you should do, but know that there are definitely some things you should avoid doing. One of the major things you should avoid while presenting is making excuses to your audience. You may be nervous or feel insecure, but it never looks good in front of an audience to make an excuse about your presentation. Never start with "I didn't get much time to prepare," or "I'm not very good at this." This is insulting to your audience, and you don't want to leave them asking why you're wasting their time. Do what you need to do, and ensure that you're prepared so that you never need to make excuses.

- ***Don't Defer Answering Questions*** – While you can be afraid to let audience questions pop up in the middle of your presentation, you really can use this to your advantage. Think of the positive, if someone has a question that means that someone was listening! Seize this opportunity! Remember the best presentations feel like conversations, so never ignore the opportunity to do anything that fosters that sense of connection between you and the audience. If you ignore their question you run the risk of missing that opportunity to interact. Seize the moment.

- ***Always Repeat Audience Questions*** – Another way to ensure that you are taking every opportunity to engage the audience, is making sure that you are repeating any audience questions. Unless microphones are available, rarely will audience members be able to hear the questions that other audience members ask. Make sure to repeat the question before you answer it. It's courteous, and buys you a little more time to think up an amazing answer to the question.

Chapter 9: Practice until Perfect

We've all heard the old adage "practice makes perfect," and the reason we all keep saying it is for the simple fact that it continues to be true! A TED talk is absolutely not something you want to go into without a serious amount of preparation. This is definitely not a fly by the seat of your pants presentation, and it should be treated with the respect and hard work that its status warrants. You are going to need to practice to give a TED worthy speech, so know there is absolutely no way around that simple fact.

The most basic ways of practicing can include repeating the speech numerous times until you've memorized it, or presenting it to your reflection in the mirror. Even better try performing the speech to a group of close friends, or a small audience before you even consider setting foot on the main stage. With every repetition your confidence in your own abilities will increase, and you'll feel more and more prepared.

If you're one of those individuals who feel you don't need the practice, keep in mind TED talks actually help speakers prepare their talks six to nine months in advance! Six to nine months during which they're expected to practice, practice, and then practice some more. From there they're asked to have a final practiced version a month from the event. During this process individuals are encouraged to seek out feedback and constructive criticism from others. While this can often be helpful, you can often receive conflicting or contradictory thoughts from different people. This is why, in order to reduce confusion and stress, you need to be very choosy about the people you solicit for feedback. Ensure that it's someone who understands your goals with this presentation, and is working to the same end you are. Try to find someone who has extensive experience presenting themselves, as they're more likely to understand the possible traps and pitfalls that even the more experienced speakers can sometimes find themselves in. Practicing frequently and thoughtfully is going to increase your confidence level, and prepare you for the task at hand. When in doubt focus on the tips below to hone your presentation, and perfect the art of practicing!

Establish a Pre-Routine

Often when people are unsure or nervous they resort to superstitions in an attempt to control what is essentially uncontrollable. Instead of focusing on this exercise in futility, why not create a routine that helps you center yourself emotionally? Take deep breaths, walk the room to establish sight lines in the audience, check your microphone, and run through your presentation. All of these things you can control (at least to a certain extent), and running through each one will better prepare you to be on stage and presenting with less worry than before. Find comfort and confidence in a routine of your own making.

Set a Backup Goal

While it can be really easy to fixate on your main presentation goal with laser focus, it can be a really good idea to have a secondary goal. Sometimes this can be effective to take some of the pressure off, and refocus your attention if things aren't going quite as planned. While we hope it doesn't occur that you find your presentation falling flat, it can sometimes occur and leave you feeling that you aren't achieving what you want to. Having a supplementary goal in mind can sometimes lessen the pressure you feel to achieve in one particular area. If you do this you can stay focused on being positive and on the top of your game, no matter what direction the talk takes.

Create Contingency Plans

Along the same lines it can be really beneficial to establish contingency plans in case things begin to go south. For many people the biggest source of anxiety is the "what ifs" of a presentation. What if my slides don't work? What if something happens and I'm short time? Planning for all reasonable possibilities will leave you feeling equipped and prepared, even if (and this is hopefully the case) you absolutely never need to use them. Running through all possible scenarios will not only relieve your worry, it will also leave you more able to think on your feet no matter what arises. There will be no unexpected scenarios if you've prepared for everything!

Chapter 10: Aim to Inspire

While TED talks run the gamut in terms of topic and intention, a large majority of them involve a certain level of inspiration. Often TED talks include a sort of call to action to the listener, a plea to do better, be happier, get more motivated, or understand your self-worth (just to name a few). Often when TED talks are most successful is when they do reach out to their audience in this manner. People want to be inspired, they want to change, and they appreciate a medium that wakes them up and calls them out.

When you're appealing to your audience you are reaching them on a deeper, more emotional connection. We all have the same basic needs: food and shelter, love and belonging, desire and self-interest, and personal development, and it is on this last level that you can really connect with your audience. Truthfully we all want to learn and grow, and most people are curious about their environments, other people, and their own capabilities. Think of how many self-help and enlightenment books are sold every year. It's because we all have a fundamental desire to have a recipe for setting and achieving goals, and finding a way to overcome our limitations. If you touch on these things then you have the makings on an amazing TED talk that people will be able to connect to.

Keep in mind too that for people who want a recipe for change, they most often want the chance to make small adjustments in their daily lives. While it can seem a little dark, as complex human beings we often battle with the questions of our life. Why do we exist? What gives us meaning? Try to offer answers to these questions, or at least present your audience with some possibilities and you're headed in the right direction. A great tactic here is to focus on framing your talk as a measurable action response, to a question that people ask themselves.

Now let me explain. Many of the most satisfying talks that TED presents don't exist merely to entertain. They exist because they are a call to action to make the world a better place. You want to let your audience know that your talk will suggest the tiny, totally doable actions they can take that will lead to large, satisfying personal benefits, as well as positively effect society as a whole. These suggestions need to be relatively easy to take on, accessible, and actually incite the change you promise. If you can do this you're definitely on to something. **Keep in mind there is no one set way to phrase these ideas. Just stay true to yourself, channel your passion, present what you're excited about, and people will be intrigued.**

Remember also that presenting this information in a way that keeps your audience revved up and excited even after your speech ends, is a great way to enhance the impact of your TED talk. Try giving concrete examples of small changes that your audience can enact almost immediately. No matter how beautiful and inspiring your message, leaving the audience with something tangible to take home and apply is something that packs a huge punch. Arm them with a change they can enact in their own lives because while inspiration is great, the application of the inspiration is worth so much more! Never be afraid in your talk to call out specific action examples. It can be as simple as placing a thought in their heads such as "Tonight think of someone who needs (fill in the blank here), and decide what you can do to help them, even in a small way." Even getting their minds turning on the subject has created change.

This awakening of their consciousness will lead the person to think slightly differently about something that may not have affected them before. Your goal essentially is to have every person you spoke to that night have an idea planted in their mind that inspires them to take action. You're looking to sow the seeds of inspiration, and with the right message and delivery, it's entirely possible!

With this goal in mind focus on your big idea and the topic you've selected, and find the message within your talk that will unify the audience. From there focus on the anecdotes, and personal and emotional situations that you've encountered, that will add the necessary emotional depth to your message. When you're aiming to inspire you always want to be connecting with your audience. This is not something you can remain detached and distant from. As we've mentioned before, but specifically in this instance, it's really important to have your central idea established clearly and concisely. Set focus on this concept is what's going to give you the clarity to edit your message to the most inspiring, moving part. If what you're saying doesn't support this message, remove it.

Keep in mind that it's absolutely integral that you make use of all the advice in this book in order to have an artfully crafted, highly focused talk that will inspire others to take action in their day to day lives. Don't go off course and don't confuse your idea. You know what you have to talk about is important; now prove it to your audience!

Chapter 11: Keep it Real

While we've established how important it is to have a clear message, and a well-crafted talk, there's another component whose importance can absolutely not be overestimated. It is so necessary while you're delivering your TED talk that you stay true to both who you are and what your message is. All the tips and tricks that we've provided for you in this book will help you hone and sharpen your performance, but never underestimate how far you can get if you are genuine and authentic with your audience.

It can often be overwhelming to try to pull out your key ideas, and where exactly your focus should be. You can feel pulled in so many different directions, and clarity can be hard to find. If this is the case, take a deep breath and ask yourself why you're doing this. What do you want to share with the audience? What would you like to hear if you were in the crowd? Often we can overthink things and our important message can get lost in all the noise. Listen to yourself, and distill the message down to its essence. You're here for a reason, and you know what you want to talk about – so just do it! Trust yourself, and let the audience see who you are. Never rely on pretense or posturing. Be yourself.

Remember also that you speak in service of your audience. It can be easy when the focus is on you to feel inflated, or lose humility, or think of the audience as merely receivers of your wisdom. Don't allow yourself to travel this path. Instead, try to distance yourself from a speaker centric view of why you're doing this presentation.

Remind yourself you want to do this talk because you have an amazing idea that is worth sharing and spreading. Keep in mind that connecting this idea with the audience is your goal, whether you make an impact on 5, or 500, audience members. Remember that you are there for the audience and not the other way around. Put aside any ideas about Facebook likes, or Twitter followers, or online shares, or books sold, and just speak directly from your heart.

Show up because you want to share what you know, and remember that being yourself is key in your presentation. If you want to make an impact, do things your way, and don't fall into the trap of feeling like you have to be like someone else, or even get the same response someone else received.

Keep in mind these tips that will help you tap into the core of why you wanted to present in the first place.

- **Tell your Story your Way** – Don't give in to the temptation to try to copy the structure or persona that another talk has had success with. This will only feel contrived to your audience, and won't ring true for you. Map out the structure of course, and you can be inspired by others, but find what works for you and make that the focus of your presentation.

- **Work the Crowd** – One of your biggest strengths is you, so get out there and work what you've got! Try chatting with conference attendees before the speech, or during meals, coffee breaks, or parties. Small talk not only gives you a better idea of your audience (and it's important to know your crowd), it also allows you an opportunity to make a connection with audience members before you even climb on stage. A favorable impression in any of these other more casual venues will carry over into your presentation, so show them who you are, and why they should root for you.

- **Remember It's Not About You** – It's important both when you're writing and delivering your speech that you don't keep thinking, "I must communicate this message." Instead think of it as a sharing of information that people would love to receive. Consider what you're doing as providing a service, and the cadence and flow of your speech should begin to feel more like a conversation that a presentation.

Conclusion: Bring It All Together

Ultimately, the mission of the entire TED talks phenomenon is to help great ideas spread. In order to make sure that your idea is one of those you need to harness your passion, find a big idea, and then look at ways in which you can communicate these ideas to a varied audience. Make no mistake that your ability to be able to persuasively and thoughtfully present your ideas is an amazing skill that will bring you that much closer to achieving your dreams.

Ultimately what you'll learn firsthand as you

become a more seasoned presenter is that talks will rise or fall on the quality of the idea, the narrative, and the passion of the speaker. It really is about substance, not just speaking style or impressive multimedia presentations. Truthfully it's easy to coach any speaker through the problems that might arise in their talk, but you have to have the raw material! Having something to say is the beginning, and if you have that as your starting point you're guaranteed success.

One of the single most important things to remind yourself of, is that there isn't only one way to present a great talk. If you have a solid idea, and you take the time to figure out a novel and interesting approach, you can make it work. Make the talk your own, be authentic, and play to your strengths, and the rest will fall into place.

In this book we've provided you with the principles and strategies that will help you transform your presentations by mining your knowledge, personal experience, and individual strengths. Know that if you have the desire, then you have something worth saying. The world needs people with big ideas more than ever, and with this book you can cultivate the communication skills to match your passion. See you onstage!

Made in the USA
Monee, IL
10 December 2019